raising a pure generation
leader's guide

JULIE HIRAMINE

with the Generations of Virtue Team

GENERATIONS
OF VIRTUE
www.generationsofvirtue.org

contents

introduction

Dear Leader,

Thank you for being willing to embark on this curriculum with parents. It's certainly challenging, but talking to kids about things like sex and purity doesn't have to be as hard as some people make it out to be! *Raising a Pure Generation* was designed to make purity training accessible and doable for parents. This is why the curriculum is so simple.

More often than not, this topic scares parents – but it doesn't need to! God is the one who told us to train our children in the way they should go (and this includes issues of purity!), so He is the one who is going to help us through it. Plus, this curriculum makes it easy for parents to dive in and start those discussions, make those media choices, and train their children to live pure lifestyles.

As a leader, you have the task of putting the parents in your group at ease and guiding them through the discussion questions. Most importantly, please pray for the parents you will be leading.

The way the curriculum works is you watch a session (each session is around 24-33 minutes), break up into discussion groups and talk about the information in the video, give attendees an opportunity to share an insight or two with the group, and then parents can go home and continue the study with their Weekly Challenge and Transforming Your Family Personal Devotional in their *Parent's Guide*.

This curriculum is designed for parents who want to engage their children – whether they are 2 or 17 – in a discussion about purity and equip them to answer God's call on their lives. It's not overly complicated, and you can facilitate the sessions almost anywhere.

customize it

The *Raising a Pure Generation* DVD Series can be used in four unique ways:

Sunday school group: This is for a group that meets on church days with your church members. While sometimes it may be a bit more time-constrained, still give ample time to pray together before and after the session. If time permits, break up into smaller groups to pray for specific issues for your group members.

Cell group/Bible study: This is for your group that meets on weekdays, typically at church or someone's home. Caters well to all parents, whether couples, single parents or mixed. Encourage your (married) youth leaders to join in on the discussions as well! To keep things fun and lively, have drinks and snacks available. Consider perusing through your DVD collection and picking clever movie clips to show for each session. This really helps break the ice! Also keep in mind: if children will be present at your study, they MUST be out of earshot. These are very sensitive topics not meant for young ears!

Moms only group: This caters perfectly to your all women's group. Includes craft ideas and other practical ideas to make this DVD series work for you! Provide fun and girly snacks and beverages that your group enjoys. Play relaxing music and be sure to provide plenty of socializing time! Also keep in mind: if children will be present at your study, they MUST be out of earshot. These are very sensitive topics not meant for young ears!

Couple's date-night study: This unique idea is for a couples-only parenting study. Oftentimes, if couples with children attend a Bible study, it is more than likely their only date night. Why not make it one to remember? Set the mood with fun music, drinks and snacks, etc. We encourage the couples to take time after the study to get away together, like going out for dessert to discuss the "Study Date" questions. This gives them the opportunity to bond over their family issues and to really TALK through these issues together.

get started

Raising a Pure Generation is fairly simple to implement. There is very little preparation on your part to get ready to kick off this study with parents. Follow the simple steps below, and you will be ready in no time:

1. Read the Curriculum Overview (see page 5) to get an idea of the content you will be covering with the parents.
2. Watch Session 1: Family Connectedness, then read through Session 1 in this guide to get a feel for what is involved in each session.
3. Watch the Bonus Material on the DVD – you may want to show some of these pieces to your attendees during the study.
4. Take a look at the material you can download at generationsofvirtue.org/rapg – you'll find printable outlines for each session, printable discussion questions, promotional flyers, and a promotional video to advertise your meetings.
5. Make the necessary arrangements for meeting space, time, and details. Things you may need: projector screen, projector, writing utensils for attendees, microphone (if your group is large). You will also want to think about how you can efficiently break parents up into smaller groups for the discussion question time.
6. Now you're ready to tell your attendees what they can expect from the sessions and what you'll be covering. Encourage parents to purchase the *Raising a Pure Generation: Parent's Guide*, which includes outlines for each of the sessions, tech tips, ideas to connect with their kids on a regular basis, and the Transforming Your Family 40 Day Personal Devotional. You can find the *Parent's Guide* at www.generationsofvirtue.org (Group quantity discounts available through Generations of Virtue).
7. Pray for your group of parents – whether you have 4 or 400 parents coming to your sessions, be sure to pray for them before and during the series.

That's it – you're ready! Check out
www.generationsofvirtue.org
for more ideas on equipping parents to empower
their children for purity.

leader's to do list

curriculum overview

Session 1: Family Connectedness
Video: 24min

- What family connectedness has to do with purity
- 4 keys parents can practice to help kids avoid high risk behavior
- Ideas to connect with your kids, even if you have a busy schedule

Session 2: Parents: Guardians of Purity
Video: 25min

- Giving kids a vision of God's love story versus what Hollywood has to offer
- How parents can step into their crucial role to guard their children's purity

Session 3: Building a Pure Foundation
Video: 31min

- How to train kids to build their lives on God's word
- Practical tips to help them develop good habits for each stage of development (birth-8, 8-12, 12+)
- Addressing chores, manners, and the motives of their hearts

Session 4: Developing Purity Muscles
Video: 27min

- Body image
- How to prepare kids to guard against pornography and inappropriate imagery
- Teaching our kids to relate to siblings in a healthy way
- Why we need to talk to kids about the "birds and the bees"
- Giving kids vision for the things God has called them to

Session 5: Media Discernment
Video: 27min

- Setting standards for romance and relationships from a young age – before kids are influenced by the media's standards
- How to teach kids to discern the messages in media
- Practical steps to guard kids from pornography
- Filtering and accountability software

Session 6: The Birds and the Bees

Video: 33min

- Why the first message kids hear about sex is the most important
- What to discuss when kids are little: proper terms for anatomy
- Addressing puberty in the 8-12 age range
- Giving "the talk" – when is the right time and what do you say?
- "The talk" and how our own past affects it
- The difference between innocence and ignorance

Session 7: Don't Awaken Love

Video: 31min

- The principle of Song of Solomon 2:7
- Encouraging kids to awaken love for the Lord instead of another person
- 4 things that awaken love too soon
- Teaching kids how to prepare for their future spouses
- Modeling a deep, thriving relationship with God as a parent
- Modeling a healthy marriage relationship

Session 8: Sacred Love

Video: 30min

- The truth about dating and relationships
- Emotional bonds: keeping your heart, mind, and body whole
- Dating versus waiting
- Word study on the Hebrew words for sex in the Bible
- How to build a relationship on the truth of God

[
"You don't choose your family. They are God's gift
to you, as you are to them.",
~Desmond Tutu
]

family connectedness

Come On In! In a world that doesn't leave us much room for being connected as a family, parents have to be very intentional about spending time together, mentoring their kids, and doing things to build relationship. This session focuses on giving parents the 4 keys to helping their kids avoid high-risk behavior. Join us as we look at ways to lay a godly foundation for your family.

 before the shop opens

- Take time to pray for those attending your group
- Watch the whole session (or as a much as you can) prior to showing it to your group. This enables you to antici-pate questions and timelines.
- Go over the Customize It, FAQs, Keys to Remember and Coffee Shop Talk Sections.

 customize it

For Sunday school groups:
After welcoming your group and showing the DVD, feel free to break up into smaller groups for the discussion questions. Depending on your time frame, you may need to select only a few people to share during the Share Your Inspiration section, or have your group members share these ideas during their small group time after their discussion questions.

Also, take a look at the recommended resources listed in the *Parent's Guide*. Do your group members have these resources? Maybe some of them have already been used and purchased. Since you're going through *Raising a Pure Generation* with members of your church, consider starting a resource library. This is a great way to share all of the fantastic resources brought to you by Generations of Virtue.

SUPPLIES/TO DO

For Cell group/Bible study:

If you're able to, give time for parents to socialize before and after the session. Encourage everyone to Share Your Inspiration, and take time before and after the session for prayer.

This session especially is a time where parents really need practical ideas for connecting as a family. Consider this: have each parent throw out some practical ideas they have to connect as a family. During your study, write these ideas down on sticky notes and post them around where you meet. Before you know it, you'll have a lot more ideas down than you'd expect! Keep these ideas handy, they'll serve as your "idea vault" in the future!

For a Moms only group:

Raising a Pure Generation has a "coffee shop" feel to it. If you don't already, offer the moms coffee, tea or cider to sip on during their time together. If your group size permits, keep all of the moms together for the discussion questions, and allow time for the moms to open up. Afterward, encourage them to break up into groups of 2 or 3 to pray together over specific issues regarding their family connectedness.

If you have a crafty group, encourage the moms to bring in supplies to make a "Family Connectedness" bulletin board for their home. Bring scrapbooking and craft supplies, and give the moms time to create an "idea board" for their family to use to encourage them to connect. Allow them time to collaborate and share ideas with one another.

For a couple's date-night study:

For this session, encourage your couples to discuss the following questions on their "Study Date":

1. For each of your kids, how do they feel loved? Remember, as the old saying goes, "Kids spell love T-I-M-E".
2. List 3 ways you want to connect as a family together this month:
   a.
   b.
   c.
3. When you are together as a family, what occupies most of your time and attention? How does that need to be adjusted?

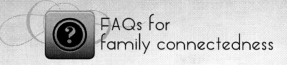

FAQs for family connectedness

1. What if I'm too busy to connect? Answer: Parents, we know how incredibly busy you are! Don't feel like the connecting has to be a huge ordeal. Look for practical, simple things you can add in to spend a little more time connecting everyday. You can also think of ways to involve your kids in your daily activities.

2. I'm a single parent. How do I connect? Answer: You can absolutely do this as a single parent. It might look a little different, but you are still the best person to connect and talk to your kids.

3. My kids don't want to hang out with me. Then what? Answer: Make sure you are choosing activities that are good for all your children. Realize the attention span of your 3 year old is going to be different than your 10 year old. If the 3 year old can't sit through family devotions, that is ok. Pick things that vary in interest for each child, and most importantly…. Stick to it!

 keys to remember

- The four keys to staying connected:
  Family Connectedness
  Expressing Expectations
  Positive Input
  A Father's Involvement
- "Rules without relationship lead to rebellion, while relationship without rules leads to confusion." Josh McDowell
- Remember: the connecting doesn't have to be elaborate. Incorporate connecting together into things you already have to do anyway.

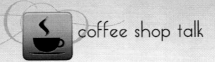

coffee shop talk

LEADER'S NOTE

Have your people share their ideas with the whole group. You never know what good ideas might be shared that can really be helpful to people. One time I (Julie) was at a Christmas cookie exchange and everyone shared a Christmas tradition their family had. I really liked what a couple people shared, and we still use those ideas today, years later, in our family.

1. In addition to the ideas that were shared with you to connect as a family, what other ideas can you think of? Maybe you're already connecting together as a family on a regular basis- that is great! What ideas can you share with those in your group to help them enhance their time together as a family? What is one new way to connect you will implement this week?

2. As parents, we seldom take the opportunity to speak with our children about issues that make us uncomfortable. We assume that they would never lie or hide a relationship from us. What about things like having sex, technical virginity, oral sex, and being physically involved with someone of the same sex; do we ever talk to our teens about the pressures that they are really facing out there in the world? We may feel uncomfortable laying out the expectations for our children, especially when it comes to things like relationships, sex, media and technology, etc. while things like behavior and manners can sometimes be spoken so easily! Besides speaking, what are some other ways you can think of to express your expectations? If you have young children, being clear about how they treat others and act with their siblings is one area to address. Are there other areas that our young kids face?

3. How do we balance the negative versus positive feedback we give our children? Is there always more positive to outweigh our nagging and negative comments? Try to make 2 positive or encouraging statements to your child for every correction or negative remark.
    *   Take a moment to jot down a few things you love about your children. Now ask yourself: do they know these things? Are they sure of my love for them, or are they so bombarded by criticism that they don't see it?

4. You, dads, are incredibly busy! (Or, if you're all moms, you know how busy your husbands are!) While culture puts so much pressure on fathers to do "the big things" like taking your kids on an expensive vacation, what are some everyday things you can do to connect with your children? Remember, dads: It doesn't have to be a big deal. But the time you spend with your children will mean the world to them as they grow up. What are some ideas that you have to incorporate your kids into the things you have to do anyway?

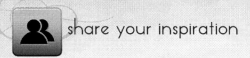 share your inspiration

Provide time for each person in your group (or if your group is large, just pick a handful) to share what they are hoping to get out of the *Raising a Pure Generation* DVD Series. What are their hopes for their children? What are they hoping is the end result of the study?

 weekly challenge

SHOT OF ESPRESSO

Give your groups plenty of time to discuss the Coffee Shop Talk questions. As the leader, be sure to have input and suggestions for each of the discussions in case a group isn't sure or gets stuck.

Everyday this week, play the game "A Rose, A Thorn and Spaghetti". This fun and easy game is perfect for the whole family, and a great way to connect together! (It makes a great dinnertime game.) Here are the rules:

Have your family sit together in a circle and ask each person to share their "rose, thorn, and spaghetti" for the day:

> **Rose:** Something good that happened today
> **Thorn:** Something bad that happened today
> **Spaghetti:** Something silly that happened today

Allow each person to share. You'll be surprised at the laughs and insight you'll get as you give each child the opportunity to share - whether they are 2 or 17!

While you're together as a family, why not take a moment to pray together? Ask your kids if they have any prayer requests and take time to come together before the throne of God. These special times are key in building family connectedness.

Need some inspiration?
Check out www.generationsofvirtue.org for resources and easy ways to connect together!

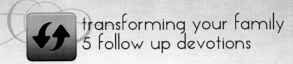

transforming your family
5 follow up devotions

LEADER'S NOTE

Pray for each member of your group every day this week. Pray that they will be committed for the entire study and that God will open their hearts to how He wants to refine and build up their families.

1. Read Deuteronomy 6: 4-9. Pray about the example you are showing your kids. Do they see from your actions, your speech, your instructions, that the Lord is your God?

    •   Wait upon the Lord and ask Him if there are any actions toward one of your children that He would want you to change. Ask Him to transform that today and throughout this week.

    •   Is there something you have said or a pattern of speaking to your kids that God needs to change? Bring this area before Him and submit it to Him.

    •   Are you intentionally instructing your kids in the ways of the Lord? Ask God to give you one idea that you can do this week with your family.

2. Read Ephesians 4:1-3. Are there any areas of tension between you and members of your family that is making it difficult to connect? Lift these areas up before the Lord and ask Him to work out these problems. As you wait on the Lord, seek Him for His divine answers to the difficulty you face today.

3. Read 1 John 2:3-6. Pray specifically about the example of obedience you give your kids. Do they see you seeking God's direction on a daily basis? Do they see you follow His direction? Ask God to show you one area He wants you to examine and work on.

4. Read Romans 7:21-25. Is there anything you see yourself doing that you don't want to pass on to your kids? Pray specifically about this issue. Ask God to sever the generational sin that gets passed down to the 3rd and 4th generation (Numbers 14:18). Ask the Lord to change the next generation and commit them to Him.

    •   Is there anything negative that was passed from your parents to you that you want to be cut off before the next generation inherits it?

5. Read Ephesians 5:15-16. Time with your family is short. Pray about ways you can make the most of the time you are given with your children. What areas of your daily life could you open up and allow your family into? Are there any things you do regularly that you can invite a kid or two to join you on?

session two:
parents: guardians of purity

["The ultimate test of a moral society is the kind of
world that it leaves to its children."
~Dietrich Bonhoeffer]

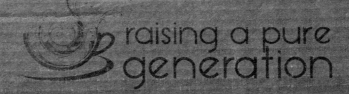

parents: guardians of purity

Come On In! If our kids are going to be able to stand against the tide of impurity in our culture, we as parents must learn to be the ultimate protectors of their purity. This session is foundational in helping you understand what it means to be your children's guardians, and how to build an impenetrable wall to protect against the forces of darkness that try to come against our children. As you participate in this session, ask yourself: how do I want my kids to be on their wedding day? How will they get there?

 before the shop opens

- Take time to pray for those attending your group
- Watch the whole session (or as a much as you can) prior to showing it to your group. This enables you to anticipate questions and timelines.
- Go over the Customize It, FAQs, Keys to Remember and Coffee Shop Talk Sections.

 customize it

For Sunday school groups:
After welcoming your group and showing the DVD, feel free to break up into smaller groups for the discussion questions. Depending on your time frame, you may need to select only a few people to share during the Share Your Inspiration section, or have your group members share these ideas during their small group time after their discussion questions.

Encourage parents to be open about their prayer requests regarding these issues. Have all of your attendees pray for the issues that one another is facing, and as prayers are answered, be sure to have your parents share those with the group!

SUPPLIES/TO DO

For Cell group/Bible study:
If you're able to, give time for parents to socialize before and after the DVD session. Encourage everyone to Share Your Inspiration, and take time before and after the session for prayer.

Let's face it: when it comes to purity and sex, it can be difficult to "chart a course" for our kids' education in this area. Consider making an age-by-age timeline to put on a big wall at your study. Have the timeline begin at age 0 and end at age 21. As parents, brainstorm ideas on how and when to talk to your kids. As a group, this begins "charting a course" for your children's purity education. Include topics you're going to cover and resources to use! With each session of *Raising a Pure Generation*, keep adding action items to the timeline. At the end of the series take a photo or have someone type up the timeline to give to each participant.

For a Moms only group:
Raising a Pure Generation has a "coffee shop" feel to it. If you don't already, offer the moms coffee, tea or cider to sip on during their time together. If your group size permits, keep all of the moms together for the discussion questions, and allow time for the moms to open up. Afterward, encourage them to break up into groups of 2 or 3 to pray together over specific issues regarding their needs in this area.

Bring supplies for each mom to create a "timeline" for her family (make sure you have plenty of rulers, paper and markers!). Have the timeline begin at the age of their youngest child, and go to age 21. Now, begin to help them shape what they want to talk to their children about at each age, especially regarding sex, purity, relationships, media and technology. What resources would they like to use? What topics do they need to cover? This encourages the moms to have an action-plan when it comes to the topic of purity without feeling overwhelmed (very common) or like failures (if they haven't talked to their kids yet). Remember: it's never too late to begin!

For a couple's date-night study:

For this session, encourage your couples to discuss the following questions on their "Study Date":

1. When do you think you should talk to your kids about sex, purity and relationships? What do you think they already know? (Consider the movies and media influence to which they have access). Is there any "un-doing" that needs to happen?

2. How did each of you find out about sex? Do you want something different for your children? Remember: you two have the chance to share the first message with your kids! YOU get to shape their view on sex, relationships and purity! (Isn't that amazing?) This is an opportunity to change the trajectory of your generational line for future generations if you did not grow up in a Christian environment or if you grew up in a dysfunctional environment.

3. What topics brought up in this session do you think you need to address with each child? When do you think you should begin these conversations? Feel free to create a timeline for how and when you're going to talk to each child, what topics you need to cover, and which resources to use!

 FAQs for
parents: guardians of purity

1. My young children are nowhere near "the relationship stage". Do I really need to be talking about this? Answer: Yes! Absolutely. At this young age you are building the convictions that will last them a lifetime.

2. My older child has already lost his or her purity, does this session address this dilemma? Answer: Yes. Even if your child has chosen a less-than-ideal path, this will equip you to help him or her while setting you free from guilt.

3. What do you mean by being a "guardian"? Don't most kids see that as being controlling? Answer: Guarding your children's purity isn't about controlling them at all. It is about helping them face these issues head on so that they are equipped for life. It's all about training them to make responsible, pure choices on their own now and in the future.

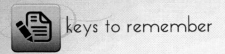 keys to remember

- The four things we need to be to guard our kids:
  Intentional
  Purposeful
  Protecting
  Persevering
- Giving our kids a love story that is better than anything Hollywood could come up with
- Even a little bit of evil can be especially harmful to our young ones' lives

SHOT OF ESPRESSO

Encourage your attendees to envision their kids as adults, maybe on their wedding day. What do you want their experiences and childhood to have been like? What do you want them to be standing for? Then ask: as parents, are you preparing them for those things right now?

 coffee shop talk

1. Having a course charted needs to start with a destination in mind. What is your goal with your kids' purity training? Meaning: regarding purity, what training and experiences do you want them to have, by, say, age 21? Discuss as a group how you can chart this course for your family.

2. You know the old saying "Fail to plan; plan to fail"? How does this saying relate to teaching your kids about sex and purity?

3. Remember the principle in the video about "experience versus knowledge"? Think of a time where either you or your children have chosen experience over knowledge. What was the outcome? Regarding sex education and purity, would you rather your children learn by experience or knowledge? Why?

4. Can you think of any way, probably completely unintentionally, that this culture has driven your family to tolerate a "little bit of evil" instead of standing against it? What appetites have been created that make your kids hungry for more?

5. How do we plant seeds that will grow into virtues in our kids?

6. What kinds of consequences do your kids experience that illustrate the principle of sowing and reaping? Specifically with teens, how can we motivate them to make good choices?

share your inspiration

Encourage each person in your group (or just select a handful if you have a large group) to share the one "key" that they learned from the previous session. What areas are they seeing growth in? This time will promote openness and honesty in your group and encouragement as they continue!

weekly challenge

As behavior issues pop up this week, take a minute to go further with your kids. Instead of just correcting the immediate issue, consider if there are things that God is nudging at that may be a bit deeper, things that may be a heart motive or intention that is not right. For instance, if your child has the habit of telling "little white lies", begin to look at the deeper root. Why are they doing this? What is their motive?

transforming your family
5 follow up devotions

The following devotions will focus on the first half of the book of Nehemiah. Each day, you will read portions from this book. As you study the scripture, relate the walls to the protection around your child's purity. Look at these next five days as a concentrated effort to see where the walls around your family's purity may be in disrepair and need rebuilding. Where has the enemy been able to attack you as a family – specifically in the area of purity - because of this disrepair?

LEADER'S NOTE

Encourage your group to engage in this devotional study to apply what they have learned this week. Pray for them each day that God will dive deep into their hearts with His word.

1. Read Nehemiah chapters 1 and 2:1-8. Nehemiah started the process of rebuilding the walls by prayer, fasting, and repenting. Begin these five days by fasting and praying. Repent of places of impurity in your own heart (whether it be past or present). Repent on behalf of your children and your spouse as Nehemiah repented on behalf of Israel.
    *   Instead of just fasting food, ask God if there is a specific kind of media He wants you to fast from and take the time you would be spending with that book, TV show, movie, website, etc. to spend time with the Lord.

- Wait on the Lord to bring an area to your mind and then spend time repenting. The Lord Himself will search out our hearts of areas that need to be surrendered to Him; even if these areas are from years past. (Psalm 19:12)

2. Read Nehemiah 2:9-20 and chapter 3. Today, assess the walls in your family. What damage has the enemy been able to do because of the disrepair? Inspect the damage and pray about how to rebuild your walls. As the Lord leads and as it is appropriate, talk to your family about the damage.
   - For instance, are there movies you've watched recently that had a negative message that has affected your children negatively? What about songs, video games, activities, etc.?
   - As the first line of defense between the enemy and your children, are there openings in your life that are allowing bad influences to come in? Ask the Lord right now what these openings are and how to repair them.

3. Read Nehemiah chapter 4. What influences are hindering your work of rebuilding the wall? Is it the culture? Friends or friend's families? Identify these influences and pray about them. Ask the Lord to protect you and your family from any nay-sayers who would have you believe it's not possible to stand for purity in our culture.
   - Ask God to give you one new idea on how to be in the world but not of it (John 17:15-16 and Romans 12:2).
   - Wait on God; an idea that is from Him will be like a light going on. It will be an "aha" moment or something like "wow, I never thought of it like this before!"
   - Think about the appetites you create in your children. Are you allowing "tastes" of things that are going to become unhealthy appetites in the future?

4. Read Nehemiah chapter 5. This chapter talks about the oppression of the poor by the officials and nobles. Apply this chapter to the members of your family. Is anyone doing something that is hindering a brother or sister in his or her walk for purity? Is there anything you are doing as a parent that is frustrating your kids, making it difficult for them to obey God's direction about purity? Ask the Lord to show you areas where oppression may be going on in your family.
   - Ask God to shine His light on relational dynamics especially between siblings. Remember, you are not just focusing on purity of body. Are there any relational dynamics that do not reflect purity of heart and mind (IE: thoughts our kids have toward one another that are just not very nice!)? Ask God to give you strategies to tackle this.

5. Read Nehemiah chapter 6. In this chapter, Nehemiah rightly anticipates and avoids a conspiracy against himself. Today, ask the Lord to show you any plots from the enemy targeted at you, specifically to distract you from the work of building walls around your family. Where is the enemy trying to intimidate you or the members of your family? Pray for freedom from fear and oppression from the enemy.

[
"Children are not casual guests in our home.
They have been loaned to us temporarily
for the purpose of loving them and instilling a
foundation of values on which their future
lives will be built.."
~Dr. James Dobson
]

raising a pure
generation

building a pure foundation

Come On In! You as parents are the gatekeepers of your home. It is up to you to determine how wide or how narrow the gate of influence is left open to allow the culture in. Sometimes it can be difficult to determine which influences will be helpful or harmful to your children in the long run. This session focuses on the tools that you as parents need in order to "guard the gate".

 before the shop opens

- Take time to pray for those attending your group
- Watch the whole session (or as a much as you can) prior to showing it to your group. This enables you to anticipate questions and timelines.
- Go over the Customize It, FAQs, Keys to Remember and Coffee Shop Talk Sections.

 customize it

For Sunday school groups:
After welcoming your group and showing the DVD, feel free to break up into smaller groups for the discussion questions. Depending on your time frame, you may need to select only a few people to share during the Share Your Inspiration section, or have your group members share these ideas during their small group time after their discussion questions.

If your group members are like most families, they are always in search of clean, appropriate, family-friendly movies. Why not create a library of clean movies for your church? Share some of your favorites or just recommend titles! A good suggestion always helps.

SUPPLIES/TO DO

For Cell group/Bible study:
If you're able to, give time for parents to socialize before and after the DVD session. Encourage everyone to participate in the Share Your Inspiration section, and take time before and after the session for prayer.

Take some time to have everyone in your group brainstorm movies that are good for families. You may even be able to loan movies back and forth between families or at least have a list of "safe" movies families can find for themselves.

For a Moms only group:
Raising a Pure Generation has a "coffee shop" feel to it. If you don't already, offer the moms coffee, tea or cider to sip on during their time together. If your group size permits, keep all of the moms together for the discussion questions, and allow time for the moms to open up. Afterward, encourage them to break up into groups of 2 or 3 to pray together over specific issues regarding this topic.

As every family knows, sometimes it takes some reminding to make the media rules stick! Bring supplies for the moms to create a "Media Values" list for their homes. Keep it fun and creative! This will help kids remember the movie, TV, video game and computer rules.

For a couple's date-night study:
For this session, encourage your couples to discuss the following questions on their "Study Date":
1. How has media affected your kids? How much have they been exposed to? In regards to their understanding of sex, purity and relationships, how has media shaped their current viewpoint?
2. How has this session changed your viewpoint on media and your kids?
3. What rules need to be put in place regarding (these may need to vary by the age of you children):
    * Movies and TV
    * Computers
    * Video games
    * Cell phones
    * Music

FAQs for building a pure foundation

1. Does being a gatekeeper when it comes to media mean that my kids shouldn't be allowed to watch anything? Answer: Not at all! Certain shows and movies are obviously not appropriate for children (or anyone for that matter!) but the goal is to help you determine what kinds of influences you want shaping your children.

2. My kids already watch programs that I disagree with. What should I do? Answer: After watching this session, sit down with your spouse and evaluate what is of value to your children. If that video game or TV program or movie has no value, then be determined to not allow it in your home.

3. Many times, extended family members are the ones who watch our children. They do not have the same values that we do, and we feel that they are influencing our children for the negative, even though they love our kids. What should I do? Answer: Prayerfully consider your position and situation before you do anything. But even within family, it is a question of influence. God has placed the responsibility of your children on you. When you stand before God, you will not be able to say, "But they were family, so I couldn't say no." If a relative is not a good influence on your child, it is up to you to protect your child in that situation, even if that means not allowing that relative(s) to babysit, etc. Also, put guidelines in place when they are visiting, as well as a way to monitor whether those guidelines are observed.

 keys to remember

-   We want the Word of God to be the foundation in the hearts of our children. Get the Bible into them at every opportunity!
-   Obedience is key, children need to have soft, moldable hearts willing to listen to the Lord.
-   Be aware of who may be influencing your kids, including babysitters, extended family members, nannies, etc.
-   Manners, especially for boys, are very important!
-   Be willing to deal with the "small things" before they snowball into huge issues.
-   Remember: No family is "normal". Normal is just a setting on the dryer!

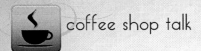 coffee shop talk

1. What ways can you get the word of God into your children? Kids like to memorize, especially when they're really young. They have such a hunger for learning at this age, so take advantage of it! What creative ideas have you used in your family to get the Word into your kids' hearts?

2. We all have times when we need a little help with the kids, whether it is a nanny or an occasional babysitter. In either instance, what are your requirements for someone being alone with your children? If you and your spouse have not already done so, consider making a list of babysitting "Do's and Don'ts". What would be on your list?

3. In our society, children are frequently excused from doing chores. Yet helping around the house and cleaning up is important for every young person to learn responsibility. How can you help your kids get more involved with the day-to-day chores? What ways have you made this successful in your home over the long run? What are your challenges?

4. Do you have creative ideas for working on manners with your children?

5. Do laptops have legs in your home? Do they wander off into quiet corners of the house or into bedrooms? Why or why not is this okay for your family?

6. What kinds of pressure do you feel to be a "perfect" family? How do you deal with this pressure?

SHOT OF ESPRESSO

If time permits, encourage parents to write out their media standards for their homes. What types of music, games and media do they want influencing their children? What is age appropriate? Keep in mind that the freedom in music, games and media usually increases as the children get older, but there should still be a strong moral ground for their choices.

 share your inspiration

Encourage each person in your group (or just select a handful if you have a large group) to share the one "key" that they learned from the previous session. In which areas are they seeing growth? This time will promote openness and honesty in your group and encouragement as they continue!

weekly challenge

This week, implement a "Manners Week"[2] – a week-long concentrated effort to practice good manners. At the beginning of the week, go over with your family the basic manners you want to practice this week. It may be saying things like "please pass the butter" at the dinner table instead of "hey – gimme the butter!", or it could involve deeper issues like cleaning up after yourself instead of expecting someone else to. Mom and Dad need to be diligent to practice good manners as well! At the end of the week, debrief with one another and evaluate how the week went. What did you learn? What do you need to keep working on?

transforming your family
5 follow up devotions

1. Read Jeremiah 29:11-13 and Isaiah 42:6. Pray today about God's calling for each of your children. Ask Him to show you and your children very clearly what His specific calling is for each one of them as they grow up.

2. Read Hebrews 11:8-11 and think about all Abraham and Sarah did in faith – not knowing why or what would come of it. Ask the Lord what He wants to put in the foundations of your children's lives. Since He knows what they will be doing in the future, He knows what is the best preparation for that future.
   - Think specifically about chores as you are praying. Are there any chores, like the laundry, that you could have your kids take responsibility for?

3. Read Romans 2: 6-8. Pray specifically about your children's areas of disobedience. Lift these issues up to the Lord and ask Him to reconcile them to Him. As you are praying for your children, lift up your own issues of disobedience. Are there areas you are seeing where your example of disobedience is hindering your children from making the right choices?

4. Read 2 Timothy 3:16, John 6:63, Psalm 119:125 and 119:130. Ask the Lord today to give you and your children an inextinguishable love for God's Word. Ask Him to help you memorize it, read it daily personally and as a family, and understand it. Ask Him to give you a verse you can write down and memorize today.

> **LEADER'S NOTE**
>
> Be praying for the members of your group everyday. Pray that God would give them vision for their family and each of their children. Pray that each family will have a foundation built on God's Word.

5. Make a list of strengths for each child. Now make a list of areas that are weaknesses they need to work through. Pray for God to show you the intents and motives of their hearts.
   - Can you identify a "romantic" in your family? How can you help this child keep love asleep while finding an appropriate outlet for those feelings?
   - Now think about your whole family – do you have a media junkie? Is the TV news on all the time at your home? Do you need to make some adjustments? What kind of time limits do you institute in your home with media?

notes

_____

_____

_____

_____

_____

_____

_____

_____

_____

_____

[
"It is easier to build strong children
than to repair broken men."
~Frederick Douglas
]

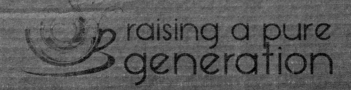

developing purity muscles

Come On In! If our kids are going to have strong values when it comes to purity, then we must begin building those muscles now, not wait until they are 15 or 16 and expect them to succeed! Think of it like this: You would never expect your teen to finish a marathon if she can barely run a mile. You would never expect your child to ace a chemistry exam if he has never taken the class. It is the same when it comes to their purity! They need to be trained and prepared so that they can stand strong for purity and holiness in today's dark world.

 before the shop opens

- Take time to pray for those attending your group
- Watch the whole session (or as a much as you can) prior to showing it to your group. This enables you to antici-pate questions and timelines.
- Go over the Customize It, FAQs, Keys to Remember and Coffee Shop Talk Sections.

 customize it

For Sunday school groups:
After welcoming your group and showing the DVD, feel free to break up into smaller groups for the discussion questions. Depending on your time frame, you may need to select only a few people to share during the Share Your Inspiration section, or have your group members share these ideas during their small group time after their discussion questions.

As a ministry, we have had countless young men and fathers express to us concern that they cannot attend church or youth group, because the outfits that the girls and women wear are causing them to struggle. Take some time to discuss modesty standards as a group. You can even outline your ideas with sticky notes.

SUPPLIES/TO DO

_____
_____
_____
_____
_____
_____
_____
_____
_____
_____
_____
_____
_____
_____
_____
_____
_____

For Cell group/Bible study:

If you're able to, give time for parents to socialize before and after the DVD session. Encourage everyone to participate in the Share Your Inspiration section, and take time before and after the session for prayer.

As a ministry, we have had countless young men and fathers express to us concern that they cannot attend church or youth group, because the outfits that the girls and women wear are causing them to struggle. As a group, you can play a huge role in turning this problem around, by setting and upholding your own standards. Encourage each family to take an honest evaluation of their modesty standards. Is there anything that needs to be adjusted?

For a Moms only group:

Raising a Pure Generation has a "coffee shop" feel to it. If you don't already, offer the moms coffee, tea or cider to sip on during their time together. If your group size permits, keep all of the moms together for the discussion questions, and allow time for the moms to open up. Afterward, encourage them to break up into groups of 2 or 3 to pray together over specific issues regarding this topic.

As a ministry, we have had countless young men and fathers express concern over the way girls dress when they attend church. As women, it is our responsibility to guard and protect the hearts and minds of the men around us by covering our own bodies. It is also so important that we teach our daughters how to value their bodies by dressing modestly. To help you get the movement started, consider hosting a modest fashion show. Pull together some fun outfits and throw a party to teach moms and daughters (and friends!) how to be trendy and modest.

For a couple's date-night study:

For this session, encourage your couples to discuss the following questions on their "Study Date":

1. For your daughters: What guidelines do you feel should be put in place as far as modesty? If she is young, are the standards you currently have acceptable to carry throughout her life? (For instance, does she wear a bikini now when she is 2? Do you want her to wear a bikini when she is 15?)

2. For your sons: Dads, you know how visual your pre-teen and teen boys are. What practical ways can you think of to help your son "bounce his eyes" when he is tempted to look at women inappropriately?

3. Think of each of your children and ask: are they comfortable with who God made them to be? Do they feel accepted and loved? How can you further encourage them as the boy or girl God created them to be? Have you given them a hug today and expressed that you love them?

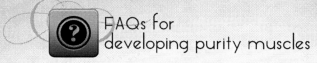

FAQs for developing purity muscles

1. My kids aren't so little anymore. Do these tips still work? Answer: Yes! Of course, there are some adjustments that will need to be made, but never believe that your kids are "too far gone", even if you're a little behind. Jump on it and put these tips into practice!

2. When it comes to modesty, my daughter and I really disagree. How do I explain why it is so important to stay covered up? Answer: Even if you have never talked to your daughter about modesty, it is never too late to start. Oftentimes girls dress a certain way to get attention, and to feel pretty or even "worshipped" for their figure. A great resource for talking with girls about this is *Secret Keeper Girl* by Dannah Gresh (for 8-13 year olds) and *Secret Keeper* by Dannah Gresh (for 13+). These are fantastic resources to give a fresh perspective on modesty.

3. My spouse and I have not modeled a healthy "God-given" love story. Are my kids doomed to fail? Answer: Absolutely not! But it will be very important that you give them a healthy perspective on what love should be.

 keys to remember

- Be sure to affirm your child's gender. They need to know that God made them perfectly, just the way they are!
- Encourage your girls to dress modestly, even from a young age
- Encourage your son to "bounce his eyes" when he comes across inappropriate imagery
- Don't forget to talk to your kids about "the birds and the bees"!
- Instill vision into your children for what God is calling them to do

LEADER'S NOTES

_____

_____

_____

_____

_____

_____

_____

_____

_____

_____

_____

_____

_____

_____

_____

_____

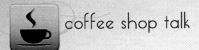 coffee shop talk

1. Can you see how our culture has put pressure on our kids that they "just aren't right" they way God made them? Whether it be their gender, sexuality, ethnicity or the like, it seems like culture's voice never stops. How can we as parents validate our children in a greater measure when it comes to how they were created?

2. Do you have modesty standards for your daughters? How did you come up with these standards? Remember: take those seemingly cute outfits ten years down the road. Are there any adjustments that need to be made to your daughter's wardrobe? (Whether she is 2 or 16!) *A note to parents: We have had an astounding number of young people tell us that they no longer attend church because of what the girls were wearing. Parents, please monitor your daughter's clothing choices. Realize that what she wears affects those around her, and her closthing choices can even be damaging to a fellow brother's faith.

3. What creative ideas can you think of to help your son guard his eyes? Whether it be "bouncing his eyes", looking down, checking his phone, etc. what ideas could be helpful for him to guard himself visually? What has worked best? No matter what age your boys are, preparing them to have victory in this battle is key. How can you begin right now?

4. When your children look at your marriage, what do they see? Are you preparing them for their amazing, God-given future? Why or why not?

5. Where do you find the most issues with your kids: books, music, technology, or experiences with friends? Share some ideas about how to counteract these issues.

 share your inspiration

Encourage each person in your group (or just select a handful if you have a large group) to share the one "key" that they learned from the previous session. In which areas are they seeing growth? This time will promote openness and honesty in your group and encouragement as they continue!

SHOT OF ESPRESSO

Especially when it comes to modesty, things can get a little sticky with our girls, and sometimes moms and daughters just need a little help when it comes to picking out appropriate clothes. Consider hosting a "Modesty Fashion Show" for moms and daughters at your home or church.

 weekly challenge

This week, set aside a time (or two) to worship together as a family. Even if you don't play any instruments, you can find worship lyrics online and sing. It doesn't have to be a super ceremonious event that takes planning and lots of time to prepare. Your worship time can be as simple as finding some song lyrics or recorded worship music, gathering the family together, singing, and then closing your time in prayer. You can also sing a worship song when you sit down to dinner and pray for the meal. If you are a musical family, invite members to play their instruments. The point is this is your time as a family to gather together and worship God for who He is – not how well you can play or sing!

 transforming your family
5 follow up devotions

> **LEADER'S NOTE**
>
> Pray for and encourage each member of your group to keep up with their devotional in the *Parent's Guide*. Sometimes they need encouragement and reminders to keep them going.

1. Read 2 Chronicles 20:15-24. Worship is a powerful tool we can use to change our situations. Spend some time worshipping the Lord before you start praying today.
    - After you are done worshipping, pray about ways you can serve together as a family.
2. Read Ephesians 6:10-18. Developing muscles is a process that requires repetition and discipline. Just like purity, it's a practice that you can't just stop and take a break from. Ask the Lord for perseverance and endurance in this battle for your family's purity. Ask God what specific battle He wants you to put on the armor of God for and fight today.
3. Read Matthew 6:33. Evaluate your personal relationship with Christ today. Before you can truly disciple your children in having a deep, intentional relationship with Christ, you must have one yourself. How do you model this love relationship with God to your kids? What areas of this relationship is He asking you to work on?
4. Read Matthew 5:22-24. Pray about your kids' relationships with one another (sibling relationships). If you only have one child, pray about your child's relationships with peers, cousins, or close friends. Do you notice points of contention that need to be worked through? Ask the Lord to show you how to help your kids learn how to use these relationships to gain practice in self-sacrifice.
    - Think about how your kids resolve conflict. Help them see the patterns they develop now will carry into their future relationships.
5. Read 1 Corinthians 15:33 and pray about the influences in your children's lives. Think about the friends with whom they are keeping company, and then think about the media with which they are keeping company. Ask the Lord if you need to sever any ties with this company.

[
"In Beverly Hills, they don't throw their
garbage away, they make it into television shows."
~Woody Allen
]

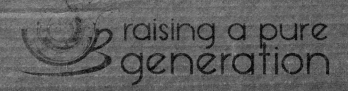

media discernment

Come On In! While many parents want to see their children successfully navigate the waves of culture, few parents realize that that training needs to begin at a young age. There will be times at every stage of your child's development that will provide opportunities for you to sow seeds of purity and holiness, especially when it comes to media discernment. Helping our kids look at media from the perspective of what is harmful versus what is of value is a process, and that can begin today.

 before the shop opens

- Take time to pray for those attending your group
- Watch the whole session (or as a much as you can) prior to showing it to your group. This enables you to anticipate questions and timelines.
- Go over the Customize It, FAQs, Keys to Remember and Coffee Shop Talk Sections.

 customize it

For Sunday school groups:
After welcoming your group and showing the DVD, feel free to break up into smaller groups for the discussion questions. Depending on your time frame, you may need to select only a few people to share during the Share Your Inspiration section, or have your group members share these ideas during their small group time after their discussion questions.

Consider opening up the discussions regarding what is and is not appropriate in TV, movies, games, etc. to your group as a whole. What does the Bible say about it? Dig deep into God's Word with your group to see where God stands regarding what we allow ourselves to watch.

SUPPLIES/TO DO

_____

_____

_____

_____

_____

_____

_____

_____

_____

_____

_____

_____

_____

_____

_____

For Cell group/Bible study:

If you're able to, give time for parents to socialize before and after the DVD session. Encourage everyone to participate in Share Your Inspiration, and take time before and after the session for prayer.

After your discussions, try putting two big pieces of paper up on the wall for everyone to see. On one, put "appropriate" and on the other, put "not appropriate". Encourage discussion that helps your group members ask what is "ok" and "not ok" when it comes to movies, TV, games, etc. What does God's Word say about it?

For a Moms only group:

Raising a Pure Generation has a "coffee shop" feel to it. If you don't already, offer the moms coffee, tea or cider to sip on during their time together. If your group size permits, keep all of the moms together for the discussion questions, and allow time for the moms to open up. Afterward, encourage them to break up into groups of 2 or 3 to pray together over specific issues regarding this topic.

For this session, have supplies available (or have the moms bring their own) to make a "Media Usage Chart". On the top, have the moms list the media mediums their families use: Movies, TV, Computer, Games, etc. Now, on the side, list each family member's name. Each day, put in how many minutes each person spends on each medium. Then at the end of the week, tally it up. What gets the most (and best) of your time? Moms, remember to include things like Facebook! The results may surprise you.

For a couple's date-night study:

For this session, encourage your couples to discuss the following questions on their "Study Date":

1. What gets the most (and best) of your kids' time everyday?
2. Should you limit the amount of media your kids are consuming on a daily basis? If so, how much time should be spent on things like movies, TV, social networking, chats, cell phones and video games?
3. As a family, what do you want the most (and best) of your time being spent on each day? To monitor this, consider doing the following activity:

Make a "Media Usage Chart". On the top, list the media mediums your family uses: Movies, TV, Computer, Games, etc. Now, on the side, list each family member's name. Each day, put in how many minutes each person spends on each medium. Then at the end of the week, tally it up. What gets the most (and best) or your time?

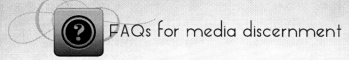 FAQs for media discernment

1. My kids have already seen inappropriate movies and TV. Is it too late? Answer: No, not at all. You may find it a bit of a struggle to "undo" some of the negative media habits that have been developed, but it's never too late to make a change.

2. I don't currently use filtering or accountability software. What do you recommend? Answer: Check out our favorites on the Technology Tools Page on generationsofvirtue.org. These are tried-and-true software recommendations that we use in our own homes. We can't say it enough times: having this software on your computer can be life-changing! It isn't worth risking your son or daughter having a lifelong struggle with pornography to not put the software on your computer.

 keys to remember

- Look to the future when you're setting standards about romance for your kids
- Use opportune moments to teach your children how media is trying to influence them
- We as parents must first be good role models when it comes to media and entertainment

LEADER'S NOTES

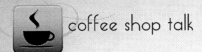 coffee shop talk

1. You as parents are the gatekeepers of your home. It is up to you how wide or how narrow that gate is left open to Hollywood's agenda. How wide or narrow is your home's gate? Why? After hearing today's session, are there areas surrounding media that need to be adjusted?

2. Have you ever met a couple who saved (or is saving) their first kiss for their wedding day? How long do you envision your kids saving their first kiss?

3. Are there any strategies you have used with your family to guard against the negative influences of TV? Are these working? What is the cue you give your family when there is something that pops up you don't want them to see?

4. Have you taken any steps to talk to your children about pornography? What ideas do you have for other parents here?

5. What kind of filtering software do you use on your computers in your home? Which software do you like? Do you find any holes in the programs you've tried?

6. Think of the programming that your children consume the most, whether it is video games, movies, music or TV. Are they teaching your children about reality and healthy relationships, or do they teach things that contradict God's Word?

7. In our world, explicit media is everywhere. The "latest and greatest" celebrity or gadget is seducing young men and women at every turn. What are some practical ideas you have to help your teens guard their eyes and hearts from these influences?

SHOT OF ESPRESSO

Parents tend to have varying opinions when it comes to how much influence they should have in their teens' lives. Feel free to allow each family to establish their own standards. Very rarely will your entire group settle on the same conclusions.

 share your inspiration

Encourage each person in your group (or just select a handful if you have a large group) to share the one "key" that they learned from the previous session. In which areas are they seeing growth? This time will promote openness and honesty in your group and encouragement as they continue!

 weekly challenge

This week, sit down with your spouse and create a media contract both for you as adults and for your family. (Take a look at the Technology Tools page on www.generationsofvirtue. org for a full list of tips and ideas to consider as you make your media contract.) Include things like:

- We commit to honoring God with our media choices, so anything that includes obscenity or sexual content, we will skip (or not watch)
- We will not watch movies with R or PG-13 ratings that have unwholesome content
- We will shut off the commercials during sports games
- We will put necessary safeguards in place on devices that can access the internet

.... you get the idea!

Our job as parents is to be an example of someone who is pursuing holiness – even in our media choices. Take this opportunity as a couple to adjust any media standards that need overhauling. We cannot expect our children to be pure if we are not! Print out your media contract and place it in prominent areas around your home. This way, everyone will know and remember the expectation. Creating this contract may mean that you will need to get rid of some of the movies you currently have in your home, and that's okay! If your kids ask you why, be sure to explain to them that you as a family are reaching for a high media standard.

 transforming your family
5 follow up devotions

1. Psalm 101:3a says, "I will refuse to look at anything vile and vulgar" (NLT). When it comes to media, are you looking at or listening to anything vile or vulgar? Are your children? How do you think "vile" media affects your thinking? What about for your children?
2. Read 2 Timothy 4:3-4. Someone once said, "Never confuse the will of the majority with the will of God." With media and our children, oftentimes the voice of Hollywood is seen as the voice of everyone. Now, you as an adult know that is not true, but do your children? Ask the Lord to show you how to teach your kids to believe the Word of God instead of the word of the majority.

LEADER'S NOTE

Ask God that the media standards of your group will be purified as they work on the devotional. Pray that there will be conviction and freedom to move toward holiness. Ask the Lord to remove condemnation so each person can pursue God.

3. Douglas Gresham, stepson of the renowned C.S. Lewis, once said "In today's world, we look at our presidents, our princes… as our leaders, but they're not. They're merely our rulers. The leaders are the people who change the minds and stimulate the imaginations of the public…That means movie makers, the people who make TV shows, the entertainment people in the business." Do you find this statement to be true? Why or why not? If it is true, who is currently the greater influence on your child: the media or you? Ask the Lord to help you influence your children the way He wants you to.

4. Many, many youth around the world have confided to us that they have seen their mother or father viewing pornography. Now, these are not non-Christian families. These are conservative parents and teens who are witnessing first hand what the porn industry is doing to families.

    • In Galatians 5:9, the Word says "A little yeast spreads through the whole batch of dough." (God's Word Translation) Our sin does not merely confine itself to one area of our lives - it permeates everything, the very nature of our being. With this understanding, is there anything in your home, on your computer, or in your heart that needs to come into the light? Pray for the Lord to bring things into the light – both in yourself and in your children.

5. Read Colossians 1:16. As Christians, we believe that God created everything and that He created everything to serve His purposes. Now, let's apply that truth to media and technology. Though sometimes it can be tempting to look at it all like garbage, how do we see it from God's perspective? What are some ways that your family can use the media, technology and resources at your fingertips to serve the Kingdom of God?

[
"Each day of our lives we make deposits
in the memory banks of our children."
~Charles R. Swindoll
]

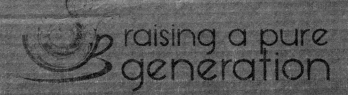

the birds and the bees

Come On In! Nothing gets parents in a cold sweat faster than bringing up "the talk". But whether your kids are 2 or 20, this subject has to be broached at some point! There are natural stages for sharing with your children about this sensitive issue with age-appropriate information. Once you are armed with the right resources and an understanding of what to actually say, you'll be ready! Remember: You as parents are the expert when it comes to you kids. By being open and willing to share with your child about sex, you are giving them God's perfect design from the very beginning, and that is an incredible gift.

 before the shop opens

- Take time to pray for those attending your group
- Watch the whole session (or as a much as you can) prior to showing it to your group. This enables you to anticipate questions and timelines.
- Go over the Customize It, FAQs, Keys to Remember and Coffee Shop Talk Sections.

 customize it

For Sunday school groups:
After welcoming your group and showing the DVD, feel free to break up into smaller groups for the discussion questions. Depending on your time frame, you may need to select only a few people to share during the Share Your Inspiration section, or have your group members share these ideas during their small group time after their discussion questions.

Nothing gets parents into a cold sweat faster than the letters S-E-X. To help break the ice, find a humorous movie clip showing a parent trying to tell their child about sex or a child

SUPPLIES/TO DO

asking a parent about sex. You can also tell a personal story along the same lines if you have one, or ask the group to tell their stories. Ask your group what their reactions are to the clip or stories shared. Can they relate? This activity will lighten the mood a little and help parents realize almost everyone struggles with the idea of telling children about sex.

For Cell group/Bible study:

If you're able to, give time for parents to socialize before and after the DVD session. Encourage everyone to participate during the Share Your Inspiration section, and take time before and after the session for prayer.

Nothing gets parents into a cold sweat faster than the letters S-E-X. To help break the ice, have your group members take turns telling humorous (yet appropriate) stories about: 1. Questions their kids have asked them regarding the birds and the bees 2. Misinformation someone told them when they were growing up or 3. Stories they have heard about questions children ask about sex. This breaks the ice and helps parents see that they really are all in this together!

For a Moms only group:

Raising a Pure Generation has a "coffee shop" feel to it. If you don't already, offer the moms coffee, tea or cider to sip on during their time together. If your group size permits, keep all of the moms together for the discussion questions, and allow time for the moms to open up. Afterward, encourage them to break up into groups of 2 or 3 to pray together over specific issues regarding this topic.

Build in some extra time to share resources that have been helpful for you or a friend regarding talking to your kids about sex. Give each mom time to share her favorite resource and why. Need inspiration? Check out the *Against the Tide* Curriculum by Generations of Virtue.

For a couple's date-night study:

Nothing gets parents into a cold sweat faster than the letters S-E-X. To help break the ice, have couples take turns telling humorous (yet appropriate) stories about: 1. Questions their kids have asked them regarding the birds and the bees, 2. Misinformation someone told them when they were growing up, or 3. Stories they have heard about questions children ask about sex. This breaks the ice and helps parents see that they really are all in this together!

For this session, encourage your couples to discuss the following questions on their "Study Date":

1.   What do you think is the appropriate age to share with your kids about topics like: sex,

oral sex, masturbation, homosexuality, etc.? How much information do you plan to share?

2. In your mind, who should be telling your kids about these topics? Why?

3. What is some information regarding sex that you found out from someone other than your parents? Was the information accurate? How did that affect each of you?

 FAQs for
the birds and the bees

1. My child seems too young for me to talk with him or her about sex. Are you sure? Answer: With the day and age that we live in, we do have to talk with our young children about sex. Now, this does not mean we have to go into every detail, but we need to be giving them age-appropriate information as they grow up. The world is different than when we were growing up, therefore we need parent differently.

2. I have older kids and did not talk with them about sex. What should I do? Answer: While it's not too late to talk with your kids, chances are pretty high that they already know how the sperm and the egg meet. Your next priority is to decipher what kind of information they received (in case you need to clarify due to misinformation) and to establish your standards and viewpoint on the subject. If your children are in their mid- to late-teens, talk with them about your expectations regarding sex, physical boundaries and relationships. At this point the discussions you will have with them will be primarily value-based.

3. I am really uncomfortable with this topic. Do you have any suggestions to help me calm down? Answer: One of the easiest ways to approach this conversation is to have resources in hand to "do the talking". There are a wide variety of resources for all ages at www.generationsofvirtue.org to help you give this all-important talk.

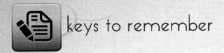 keys to remember

- It is critical that you give the first message about sex to your children.
- There is no magic age, be willing to listen to the Lord's leading for each of your kids.
- Use proper body names for private parts; this makes your job easier in the long run!
- Don't let your past hinder you from talking with your kids.

 coffee shop talk

1. How did you first learn about sex? In the long run, can you see how that shaped your attitude toward it?

2. Have you already talked to your children about sex? Did you use any resources? What advice can you offer to others?

3. How has your past hindered you from wanting to tell your children about sex?

4. What is your biggest fear when it comes to talking to your kids about sex?

SHOT OF ESPRESSO

Most parents get pretty nervous when talking to their kids about sex, and understandably so. It's a HUGE topic! To help you calm down a bit, practice reading your chosen resource aloud to your spouse. Repeat as necessary until the words become more memorized than shocking.

 share your inspiration

Encourage each person in your group (or just select a handful if you have a large group) to share the one "key" that they learned from the previous session. In which areas are they seeing growth? This time will promote openness and honesty in your group and encouragement as they continue on!

weekly challenge

This week, take some time with your spouse to discuss each child's sex education and purity training. Outline which resources you want to use with each child, what they are ready to hear, etc. Develop an outline for when you are going to talk to each child about things like:

- Body parts
- Sex
- Dating and relationships
- "The Swimsuit Lesson"

…. And whatever else you want to address!

Check out the *Against the Tide* purity curriculum from Generations of Virtue. It is an age-by-age guide to the key resources for talking with your kids about sex and purity from preschool through 8th grade. Also, feel free to visit www.generationsofvirtue.org for recommendations for your family on these key topics.

transforming your family
5 follow up devotions

1. Sometimes our past can keep us from sharing openly with our kids about sex. Is this the case for you? Do you carry baggage and condemnation from your sexual past? Friends, this is not from the heart of God. Romans 8:1 tells us "There is therefore now no condemnation for those who are in Christ Jesus." (ESV) Are you willing to lay that pain at the foot of the cross? Spend time asking God to take this baggage from you.

2. Talking to your kids about sex should involve more than a discussion about physical purity. Ask the Lord to show you the struggles that your kids face with purity of mind and heart. Pray over these areas.

3. Read Proverbs 22:6. You as parents have a unique opportunity to shape your children's view of their sexuality. You can pour in as much or as little as you want into this critical area of their lives. Ask God to help you map out here what steps you will take in the coming months to talk to your kids about the areas discussed in the DVD.

> **LEADER'S NOTE**
>
> Really keep your group members in prayer this week, as this subject is many times the most challenging for us as parents.

4. If you could tell your children one thing about staying pure, what would it be? Why? Write it down here and pray about ways to communicate this principle to them.
   • Remember that innocence does not equal ignorance.
5. What did your parents tell you about sex? How would you have changed that? What did media tell you about sex? Was it accurate or truthful? Who was the most influential voice in your life when it came to sex?

[
"Patience is the companion of wisdom."
~St. Augustine
]

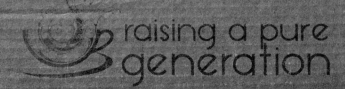

raising a pure
generation

don't awaken love

Come On In! Most young people are in search of the world's greatest love story. They want to be whisked off their feet into a fairy-tale, Hollywood-style romance. But as parents, we know the reality of love, dating and marriage. We know the incredible journey that God Almighty is setting before them, and that God's love stories blow culture's out of the water! But how do we communicate our values about love and romance in a way that illuminates God's path and fades the glowing lights of Hollywood? Let's take a look at how to equip our kids to not awaken love until its time.

 before the shop opens

- Take time to pray for those attending your group
- Watch the whole session (or as a much as you can) prior to showing it to your group. This enables you to antici-pate questions and timelines.
- Go over the Customize It, FAQs, Keys to Remember and Coffee Shop Talk Sections.

 customize it

For Sunday school groups:
After welcoming your group and showing the DVD, feel free to break up into smaller groups for the discussion questions. Depending on your time frame, you may need to select only a few people to share during the Share Your Inspiration section, or have your group members share these ideas during their small group time after their discussion questions.

After you watch the DVD, have your parents write letters to each of their children. Encourage the group to find the prom-ises of God in Scripture, verses like Jeremiah 29:11. Have the whole group look up and write these verses down on a big

SUPPLIES/TO DO

_____

_____

_____

_____

_____

_____

_____

_____

_____

_____

_____

_____

_____

piece of paper or dry erase board. This way the group can pick and choose the verses they want to include in their letters. Next, have the parents write their letters, with the intention of awakening love for God in their children by writing to them about His great love for them.

For Cell group/Bible study:

If you're able to, give time for parents to socialize before and after the DVD session. Encourage everyone to participate in the Share Your Inspiration section, and take time before and after the session for prayer.

After watching the DVD, set up two big pieces of paper on the wall and ask: What are the advantages and disadvantages of dating before you can pursue a marriage relationship? Allow the parents to discuss the pros and cons both for their own families and our society as a whole.

For a Mom's only group:

Raising a Pure Generation has a "coffee shop" feel to it. If you don't already, offer the moms coffee, tea or cider to sip on during their time together. If your group size permits, keep all of the moms together for the discussion questions, and allow time for the moms to open up. Afterward, encourage them to break up into groups of 2 or 3 to pray together over specific issues regarding this topic.

For young people, sometimes it is difficult to know what to do with your teen years if you're not going to pursue a romantic relationship until you're older. As moms, get together and think of things that your kids can do with their time instead of investing in a romantic relationship. How do you want them spending their time, efforts, and energy? Take time to really get practical. This list will be very helpful when your kids reach the age when most of their friends are "boy crazy" or "girl crazy".

For a couple's date-night study:

For this session, encourage your couples to discuss the following questions on their "Study Date":

1. What do you see as the advantages and disadvantages of pursuing a romantic relationship before you can get married?
2. In your personal lives, think of the relationships that you pursued prior to your marriage relationship. Were those helpful or harmful?
3. Still thinking about those experiences, would you want your children to experience those same situations? Why or why not? If no, what will you do to try and guide them differently?

 ## FAQs for don't awaken love

1. My child is a romantic. How do I deal with this while "not awakening love"? Answer: This can be a tough one! You don't want to squelch their love of romance forever, but at the same time, that desire needs to be put to sleep until the time is right. Especially with your romantic kids, watch the media influences that are encouraging their behavior. Whether it's a song, movie or TV show, media is oftentimes the driving force behind their desire. Oftentimes romance is a concept of sincerity and thoughtfulness. But if your children awaken romantic love before the time is right, they will just continue to be frustrated until that desire can be fulfilled in marriage. For our children, this is the time to awaken love for God, not other people.

 ## keys to remember

- 4 keys that influence awakening love too soon: TV/movies, books, music and friends
- Their 5 closest friends will influence them the most after parents
- Use their teen years to awaken a deep love for God

 ## coffee shop talk

1. How do you encourage your kids to fall in love with the Lord? Share your ideas with the group.

2. Hollywood sure throws a lot of pressure at our kids when it comes to love stories. How do we as parents give them a vision for a love story that is greater than what culture promises but doesn't deliver? How do we balance the idea of marriage ending in "happily ever after" with reality? How do we balance Hollywood's physical manifestations of "love" with the reality of God's love?

3. What is the area your kids struggle with the most: books, screen media, songs, or friends? How can you help them fast and creatively substitute different genres that put romance back to sleep?

4. When we take a peek into our own marriages, we can see the benefit of sacrificial love. Sacrificial love is a concept that can be learned even in our youngest children. What are three ways you can think of to help your children live sacrificially now to prepare them for their future spouses?

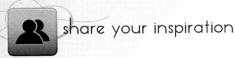 share your inspiration

Encourage each person in your group (or just select a handful if you have a large group) to share the one "key" that they learned from the previous session. In which areas are they seeing growth? This time will promote openness and honesty in your group and encouragement as they continue!

 weekly challenge

As parents, come together and discuss the "awakening love" factor in your homes. Just as we've been discussing, awakening love too soon is often influenced by movies, TV, music, books and friends. Can you see how these mediums have influenced your kids? Take a look at the main categories again:

- **Movies/ TV:** What are your kids' favorite shows and movies? Are these helpful or harmful? Are there any in your home you need to get rid of?
- **Books:** Especially with romance novels and love stories, what are your kids' favorites? Do you know the content they are reading at home? At school?
- **Music:** Who are their favorite artists and what do they stand for? Are you familiar with their lyrics? Are they "romance" driven?
- **Friends:** Are your kids' friends boy/girl crazy? Are they keeping love asleep or determined to wake it up?

Now consider: What areas need to be adjusted in order to keep romantic love asleep in your children until the time is right?

> **SHOT OF ESPRESSO**
>
> If your group is comprised predominately of families with younger children, we highly recommend *The Princess and the Kiss* and *The Squire and the Scroll* by Jennie Bishop. These books are fantastic resources to use as tools to share the concept of purity with younger ones. Both of these resources also have study guides and make excellent additions to a church or community library. You can find them all at www.generationsofvirtue.org

transforming your family
5 follow up devotions

LEADER'S NOTE

Really keep your group members in prayer this week, as this subject is many times the most challenging for us as parents.

1. Ponder Song of Solomon 2:7, which urges us "not to awaken love until the time is right." (NLT) How do you feel this applies to your own children? When do you feel the time is right?
   - If the time our kids spend with us growing up prepares them for marriage, what are you doing right now to prepare them? What have you learned today about preparing your kids for marriage?

2. For each of your children individually, what influences awaken love too soon in them? How can you come alongside them to disciple them through this? Ask the Lord to show you areas where love is being awakened in your family.

3. Read 1 Timothy 4. It is normal for your kids to have crushes. As they get older, sometimes the crushes go from "That person is really cute" to "I really want to date that person!" Those are normal feelings that every parent deals with in their teens. Think through how you will handle the crushes your children have. How will you respond? Ask the Lord to show you how to help your children apply the instruction from 1 Timothy 5:2.

4. Read Proverbs 11:2. As your children grow, they will deal with and process the various issues that all teens face. The question is not whether they will deal with them, but whether they will feel comfortable talking with you as they are walking through it. Today, think of and pray about three ways you can become a more approachable parent.

5. Read Hebrews 13:4. Children in this day and age are hard-pressed to find examples of godly, loving relationships. Instead of passion, they see pain. Instead of intimacy, they see adultery. Are you modeling the kind of relationship that your child will look at and say, "I want to be married someday?" If there are issues in your marriage that are not positive, pray about these today. Pray for God to bring unity. Also pray for your child's future spouse.

["Give God the pen [to your love story].
The single reason He gave us the pen was
so that we could give it back to Him."]
~Eric and Leslie Ludy

sacred love

Come On In! We all want our children to succeed in the area of relationships. But let's face it: The way culture tells us to go about things hasn't really worked out the last few decades. In spite of the culture, though, we are seeing young people all over the world who are striving for a different standard and are committed to walking out pure relationships in God's timing. So what do these relationships look like, and how does it all work? Let's dive in to see what sacred love is all about.

 before the shop opens

- Take time to pray for those attending your group
- Watch the whole session (or as a much as you can) prior to showing it to your group. This enables you to anticipate questions and timelines.
- Go over the Customize It, FAQs, Keys to Remember and Coffee Shop Talk Sections.

 customize it

For Sunday school groups:
After welcoming your group and showing the DVD, feel free to break up into smaller groups for the discussion questions. Depending on your time frame, you may need to select only a few people to share during the Share Your Inspiration section, or have your group members share these thoughts during their small group time after their discussion questions.

For this session, set up a big piece of paper on the wall or use a dry erase board and ask: What does a sacred love story look like to you? What aspects are the most important? Feel free to call it whatever you want, it doesn't have to be "sacred love". But the idea is: if kids are going to set a high standard when

SUPPLIES/TO DO

_____

_____

_____

_____

_____

_____

_____

_____

_____

_____

_____

_____

_____

_____

it comes to relationships, they need something to reach and strive for. What aspects should be included in a sacred love story? Take everyone's ideas and jot them down. Give everyone the opportunity to formulate their idea of a sacred love. Remember, just like everyone's love story is different, God will place convictions on every family's heart that will be unique.

For Cell group/Bible study:

If you're able to, give time for parents to socialize before and after the DVD session. Encourage everyone to participate in the Share Your Inspiration section, and take time before and after the session for prayer.

Find (or ask your group members to find) lyrics for some of the most popular songs among young people right now. Print these lyrics out and bring them to your cell group. Discuss the lyrics together. What is the artist talking about? What is he or she trying to promote? What effect do you think the lyrics have on this generation? Even if your group members' children don't listen to these songs themselves, how might their peers having listened to these songs affect them?

For a Mom's only group:

Raising a Pure Generation has a "coffee shop" feel to it. If you don't already, offer the moms coffee, tea or cider to sip on during their time together. If your group size permits, keep all of the moms together for the discussion questions, and allow time for the moms to open up. Afterward, encourage them to break up into groups of 2 or 3 to pray together over specific issues regarding this topic.

For this session, set up a big piece of paper or dry erase board and ask: What does a sacred love story look like to you? What aspects are the most important? Feel free to call it whatever you want, it doesn't have to be "sacred love". But the idea is: if kids are going to set a high standard when it comes to relationships, they need something to reach and strive for. What aspects should be included in a sacred love story? Take everyone's ideas and jot them down. Give everyone the opportunity to formulate their idea of a sacred love.

For a couple's date-night study:

For this session, encourage your couples to discuss the following questions on their "Study Date":

1. When it comes to your children's future relationships, what would be your ideal for a sacred love story?
2. If your kids are going to reach for something "bigger and better" than what the world offers regarding relationships, they are going to need a vision for what a God-orchestrated love story looks like. Who currently shapes the way they view relationships? Is it

Hollywood, the radio, God, you as parents, etc.? When it comes to love, who are they listening to?

3. When pondering your family's version of a sacred love story, what aspects are non-negotiable? Without being "militant" about it, what do you expect from your kids when they are in a relationship?

4. When do you think that relationship should begin? For instance, will you allow your children to date at 15? 18? 21? When they pursue a relationship, what should their boundaries be, physically, emotionally and spiritually?

 FAQs for sacred love

1. My children are committed to not dating. However, all of their friends are dating. What do you suggest? Answer: Standing strong in purity when all of their friends are off dating can be really tricky. Outside of your children finding a new group of friends, there are a few things we suggest. First, try to find at least one friend who is on the same page as your children. Secondly, you as parents will need to be their strongest ally. Keep encouraging them. You don't have to bash dating to encourage them to wait, be willing to talk through their frustrations and be supportive!

2. My child is really determined to date. What should I do? Answer: Well, ultimately, if your child is in your home, then he or she is subject to your rules. But that doesn't mean your teen may not push the limits. Our suggestion for this is two-fold: First of all, make your expectations clear, but don't negate your child's feelings. If your children have romantic interests, don't tell them, "Oh, you aren't in love!" or "It'll go away!" Because to them, this is a very real feeling. You don't want to alienate yourself by invalidating their feelings. Be willing to talk, and talk and talk some more! Encourage them to hear from God about this particular issue, and help them guard their hearts by not alluding to a future relationship or a crush.

DO NOT tease your child about his or her crush. Ever. Secondly, encourage hanging out in groups versus one-on-one time. If your child's crush is a member of his or her group of friends, make your expectations clear about being alone together, physical activity, etc. If this person is not a member of your child's group of friends, don't panic if they hang out in a group, but be constantly talking and checking in to make sure their actions are "above board". Most of all: PRAY!

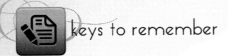

keys to remember

- Teens all over the world are reaching for a high standard, even saving their first kisses for their wedding day
- Changing the mentality of relationships from dating to waiting for God's sacred love story
- Relationships and emotions bond us to those we are in relationship with, so it is important to be in the right one

coffee shop talk

1. When do you think you should begin talking with your children about love and relationships? After listening to this session and this series as a whole, has the information changed your timeline for these discussions?

2. Do you think culture has changed the way relationships need to evolve? For instance: because of all of the dangers, are dating and casual relationships less safe/beneficial than in times past?

3. When it comes to your children's sacred love story, do you trust God with the "pen" to their love stories? Why or why not?

4. If you have younger children, how can you begin to prepare their perceptions of a sacred love story now?

share your inspiration

Encourage each person in your group (or just select a handful if you have a large group) to share the one "key" that they learned from the previous session. In which areas are they seeing growth? This time will promote openness and honesty in your group and encouragement as they continue working with their children after this study is over!

weekly challenge

Relationships can be one of the stickiest subjects for any family, so it is important to have a plan, a sort of "course charted" when it comes to how you and your spouse are going to handle the million dollar question: To date or not to date? But how?, you might ask. Well, try the ideas below to get you started. But whatever you do, remember to keep breathing, don't panic and know that God is on your side!

SHOT OF ESPRESSO

Sometimes it's hard to believe that a sacred love story really can exist in today's society. If your parents need a little incentive to believe you, head over to www.generationsofvirtue.org/cultureshock for video testimonies from real youth on the Generations of Virtue team who are committed to a God-written love story.

- Check out the resources available! Books like *Choosing God's Best* by Dr. Don Raunikar and Joshua Harris's *I Kissed Dating Goodbye* give a great perspective (these and many more are available at generationsofvirtue.org)
- Prayerfully establish your view on future relationships: Will you encourage dating? What age will your children be allowed to pursue a relationship? What will the "requirements" be?
- Prayerfully establish your expectations for your children regarding their physical purity. And be specific. Do you expect them to be virgins on their wedding day? Do you expect your kids to refrain from sexual contact? Remember, there is a lot of ground to cover between handholding and sex[3]. Where do you expect the line to be drawn?

By establishing your desire for your children's future relationships, you're helping them build godly convictions for a pure future.

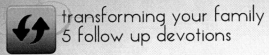

transforming your family
5 follow up devotions

1. Read Galatians 5:1. Like we talked about in this session, bonding happens at a variety of levels. Can you see times in your own life when you have been bonded to someone of the opposite sex who was not your spouse? During this session, and during your prayer time now, are there any bonds from your past that the Lord wants to set you free from? Surrender what He brings to your mind to Him completely.

2. It is said that children inherit their view of relationships from their parents. How does that saying affect you? Was that true for your situation? Outside of marriage itself, what taught you the most about relationships? Oftentimes it is helpful to take a look at our own view so that we are able to see what we are passing onto our children. Go back and read Deuteronomy 6:1-9 and seek to pass on a godly heritage to the next generations.

3. Since you have gone through the *Raising a Pure Generation* DVD Series, how has your view on dating and relationships evolved? In the future, what will your role be in your children's relationships? Write down 3 commitments in this arena of dating and relationships that God is impressing upon your heart.
    •   What is one of God's standards that you are already holding with your teens when it comes to relationships?

4. Read Psalm 46. Teaching our kids "Yada" when the world is constantly throwing "Shakab" in their faces can be a pretty difficult thing to do. But as we grow deeper in our personal relationship with Jesus Christ, as we have "yada" with Him, our teaching then becomes by example. What areas in your walk with Christ is He prompting you to let go of the old and draw closer to have "yada" with Him?
    •   What's on the menu at your house? Is there a love for God created and an appetite for Him, or an appetite for things of the world?

5. What is one thing the Lord taught you through this DVD series that you always want to remember? Write it down here. Now think of one thing you learned about love, purity, and relationships that you want to tell your children. (You could write your "one thing" to your children and mail it "snail mail" to them. Let it serve as a reminder for how your family is going to walk pure in heart, pure in mind and pure in body.)

closing up shop

If this is your final week of meeting, prepare for some kind of closure activity. If you have the flexibility to meet for week 9, you can have a time of wrapping up *Raising a Pure Generation* then.

1. Have each member of the group share one or two concepts that they have learned that has impacted their family.
2. Have each member share something they have incorporated into their family in the last 8 weeks that has made a positive difference.
3. Have each member share one thing they are going to incorporate into their family in the coming month or year.
4. If time permits, ask each parent to write a letter to their family for each child individually that expresses that Mom or Dad (or both!) is praying for their future spouses to walk in holiness before the Lord, being pure in mind, pure in heart and pure in body. Then put the letters in the mail. Kids always enjoy receiving a letter in the mail!

If your group is large, break up into groups of 5-8 to complete the closure activities. Ask if there are any group members, now that they have completed the *Raising a Pure Generation* DVD Series, that would like to lead another group of moms, couples, or cell groups in the study. Help facilitate them reaching out to more couples and families with this message.

If you are able to meet for an additional week, make week 9 a celebration meeting of completing the curriculum. Have everyone bring dessert or do a special activity together. Put up any big brainstorming papers you've worked on during the study around the room for decoration. Also make certain that someone writes up all the good ideas that your group has come up with and pass them out to the group members. Take a picture of your group and give a copy to each member with a reminder to pray that each of their children will be pure in body, mind and heart. It makes a difference when we are all praying!

Don't forget to post all the great ideas your group came up with on the Raising a Pure Generation website:

www.generationsofvirtue.org/rapg

We want all the groups going through the curriculum to benefit from what God has revealed to your group. Remember: Raising a generation to be pure is God's idea, and He is backing us all up!

endnotes

Session 1

The statistic Julie mentioned in the video about girls being 250% more likely to engage in sexual behavior if their fathers are not involved with them on a predictable basis hails from:
Society for Research in Child Development, "Fathers Respond To Teens' Risky Sexual Behavior With Increased Supervision". ScienceDaily, (2009, May 21).
http://www.sciencedaily.com/releases/2009/05/090515083700.htm

Session 2

The quote mentioned in the video comes from *Moral Revolution: The naked truth about sexual purity* by Kris Vallotton and Jason Vallotton. Destiny Image Publishers: 2010.

Session 3

[1.] We originally got the idea of "Manners Week" from Dennis and Barbara Rainey, who talk about it on their radio program, FamilyLife Today.

Session 4

From the video: The idea of using your family relationships as training for marriage originally came from Eric and Leslie Ludy, who expand upon the concept in their book, *Teaching True Love to a Sex-at-Thirteen Generation*. Thomas Nelson: 2005.

Session 5

From the video: The concept of Digital Natives and Digital Immigrants is taken from "Digital Natives, Digital Immigrants" by Marc Prensky. *On the Horizon* (MCB University Press, Vol. 9 No. 5, October 2001)
http://www.marcprensky.com/writing/Prensky%20-%20Digital%20Natives,%20Digital%20Immigrants%20-%20Part1.pdf

Session 6

[1.] The statistic mentioned in the video about 1 in 3 girls having been molested by age 18 is taken from "Child Safe Tips" http://childsafetips.abouttips.com/child-molestation-statistics.php

[2.] The inspiration for the phrase "innocence is not ignorance" in the video originally came from Dennis and Barbara Rainey's radio series entitled "Beyond Abstinence". FamilyLife Today, 1997.

Session 8

[1.] The statistics mentioned in the video about the age of initial dating was taken from Josh McDowell and Dick Day's *Why Wait: What you need to know about the teen sexual crisis*. Thomas Nelson Publishers: 1994

[2.] The word study mentioned in the video referring to yada and shakab comes from *What Are You Waiting For?: The one thing no one ever tells you about sex* by Dannah Gresh. WaterBrook Press: 2011.

[3.] This phrase is taken from *Passport 2 Purity* by Dennis and Barbara Rainey. FamilyLife Publishers, 2006.

A WORD ABOUT GENERATIONS OF VIRTUE

The mission of Generations of Virtue is to equip parents, churches, schools and organizations to empower the next generation to be pure in our world today. Generations of Virtue isn't just a ministry - it's a movement to turn the tide of culture. Starting in 2003, GOV was founded by Julie Hiramine out of a realization that parents are facing a world that is intent on trampling their children's purity of heart, mind and body. Parents need to be prepared to train their kids to stand against this force from the enemy as they answer God's call on their lives. The questions are everywhere:

- How do we live lives of purity and integrity?
- How do I talk to my kids about sex?
- How do we equip our children to choose purity instead of the cheap imitation that this world has to offer?
- How can this generation see the Living God and His incredible plan for their lives?

Generations of Virtue is passionate about providing the latest, cutting-edge resources, dynamic teaching sessions and engaging tools that groups, churches, parents, teens and families can use to stand pure before God in heart, mind and body.

For upcoming events, practical resources, and to join the movement of raising up a holy generation, visit our website: www.generationsofvirtue.org

Visit Us Online!

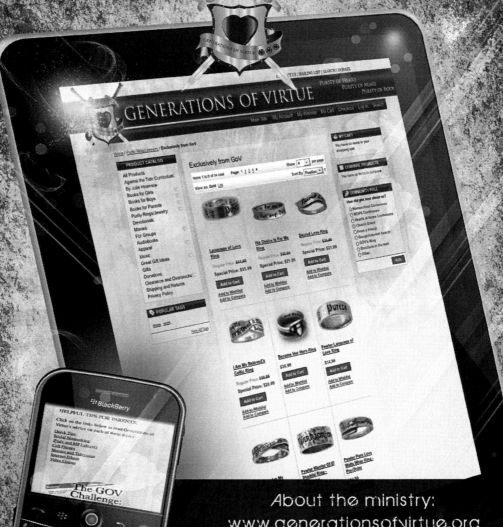

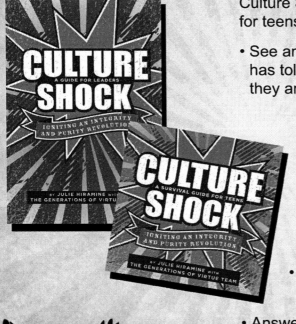

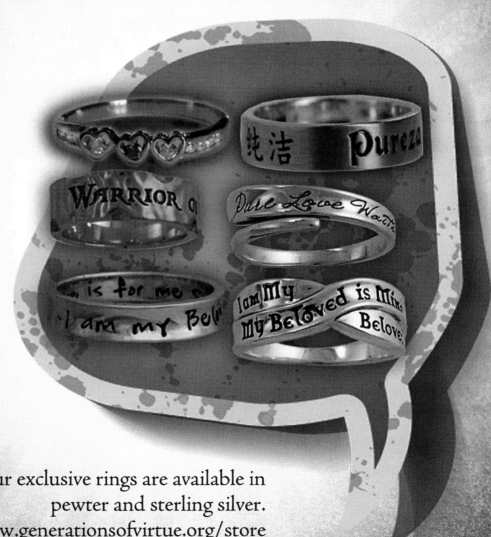

AGAINST THE TIDE

In today's world, purity training needs to start young. *Against the Tide* makes it easy for parents to engage their children in conversations about sex education, character building, and relationships using the best resources on the market. This year-by-year guide gives parents a game plan to go through our top recommended resources, along with follow up discussion questions, tips and pointers we've found from using these resources ourselves. Makes an excellent addition to your church library.

Versions available:
Against the Tide Preschool – 4th Grade
Against the Tide 5th-8th Grade